Anonymous

Under the yellow Flag

An Account of some Experiences of Henry Leffmann as Port Physician of

the Port of Philadelphia

Anonymous

Under the yellow Flag
An Account of some Experiences of Henry Leffmann as Port Physician of the Port of Philadelphia

ISBN/EAN: 9783337144296

Printed in Europe, USA, Canada, Australia, Japan

Cover: Foto ©ninafisch / pixelio.de

More available books at **www.hansebooks.com**

Under the

Yellow Flag

An Account of
Some Experiences of

HENRY LEFFMANN

as Port Physician of the
Port of Philadelphia

To which have been added a Few
Notes and Comments on the History
of the Port of Philadelphia

Printed for Presentation Only

1896

PREFACE

❧

I HAVE expressed my opinions freely in the body of the text;
it remains merely for me to record my obligations to those who
have assisted me in the preparation of the book. To Mr. Edward R.
Sharwood, Mr. Frank H. Taylor, Messrs. P. Blakiston, Son & Co., of
Philadelphia, and Mr. John M. Rogers, of Wilmington, I am indebted
for the loan of valuable cuts. I am also indebted to Mr. Sharwood
for much miscellaneous information from the files of The Philadelphia
Maritime Exchange.

In the preparation of the historical data I have been much assisted
by Mr. Jordan, of the library of the Historical Society of Pennsylvania, and Mr. Samuel, of the Ridgway Branch of the Philadelphia
Library.

H. L.

ROBERT E. PATTISON
Governor of Pennsylvania, 1883-87; 1891-95

Introductory

Cum omnis res ab imperatore delegata intentiorem exigat curam

N the 10th of November, 1884, the Honorable Robert E. Pattison, then Governor of Pennsylvania, appointed me Port Physician for the Port of Philadelphia for the unexpired term of Dr. Robert H. Alison, resigned. This office has existed for nearly two centuries as a State appointment, but its scope has varied somewhat. One of the earliest incumbents was Dr. Thomas Graeme, who held the office for many years. Dr. Benjamin Rush held it in 1790. About the beginning of the present century a Health Law was enacted and made operative for a limited period, and again re-enacted; but in 1818 this law was passed finally and has with some modifications continued in force to the present day. It established a rather peculiar arrangement of duty for the Port Physician. I was in the habit of telling my friends that my office was of such a character "that just as soon as there is anything to do, somebody else does it;" for the Port Physician's term of service was from the 1st day of October until the 31st of May, including the seasons of the year in which there is the least danger of quarantinable diseases. From June 1st until the 30th of September the inspection was done by the Lazaretto Physician, who occupied a station on the Delaware River about thirteen miles below the city. All vessels subject to inspection by the quarantine laws stopped at this station, and the office of Port Physician was practically a sinecure during these four months. The Health Law of 1818 also provided for an officer termed "Quarantine Master." The intention was to place at the station some one familiar with nautical affairs, to advise and assist the physician in examining and detaining ships. The office, however, soon became merely nominal as regards its duties. The grave responsibilities of the station necessarily devolved upon the medical officer and, excepting attention to certain routine duties prescribed by the Board of Health—such as seeing that the flag of the station "was taken down at sunset and neatly folded away," and superintending the discipline of the boat's crew—the Quarantine Master became of little importance. Even the supervision of the crew became entirely nominal, for when steam was introduced as the motor the vessel passed into the jurisdiction of the United States, the laws of which require a licensed pilot to be always in charge. The growth of political methods soon affected the question, and for many years it was an unwritten law that the appointee should be a resident of the county in which the station was located.

When I entered upon my duties in November, 1884, I was quite unfamiliar with the office. I had been appointed, without any solicitation on my part, upon the recommendation of Dr. Roberts Bartholow, who had been tendered the office, but had been obliged to decline owing to the exigencies of his professional duties. I was much gratified by the general expression of approval of the appointment by newspapers and professional friends. On assuming the office I quickly found that I had entered upon a duty offering much interest and variety, in agreeable contrast to my usual work. The medical features of the position were comparatively trifling, for as I have just remarked the serious questions of quarantine management arise during the summer season and at that period I was relieved from duty. I found that those connected with the business of the port had become so accustomed to this condition that the Port Physician did not usually appear at his office for more than a few hours each day, and never

came on Sundays or holidays except to meet passenger steamers. I
soon began to take an interest in giving to the work all the time
that I could spare from my teaching duties. I was superseded by
Dr. William H. Randle on October 4, 1887. When I relinquished
my duties, nothing was further from my thoughts than that I should
ever enter the service again. The election of a Democratic Governor
in Pennsylvania had been the event of a generation, and it would
have been considered the wildest prophecy for any one to have said
that Mr. Pattison would succeed General Beaver. In the early part of
the year 1891 Governor Pattison sent my name to the Senate as a
successor to Dr. Randle. I took the oath of office for the second
time in June of that year. I found, however, that the office was no
longer attractive. My professional duties had considerably increased;
the Board of Health had been thoroughly absorbed into the Department of Public Safety and become but a wheel in that vast political
machine which dominates Philadelphia as all American cities. The old
Board, at least partially independent of the local government, had
a freer spirit, and my relations had been very agreeable. The Bullitt
Bill had reduced the Board to five members dependent upon the
Mayor for their appointment and subject to the Director of Public
Safety. It was never clear to me how far the Port Physician was
subject to the same jurisdiction; but as time went on, my feeling of
dissatisfaction due to a consciousness of subordination increased and
I saw it was better to leave the office. In October, 1891, I tendered
my resignation, but was induced to withdraw it, to again tender it in
September, 1892.

I had at one time intended to write a history of the quarantine
service of the Delaware River and Bay, but I found that Dr. Robinson, for many years Lazaretto Physician, had published in the *Hatboro
Public Spirit* a series of articles covering a considerable portion of
this history. These articles have never appeared in book form, but a
few scrap-book copies were made up by the author. I have availed

myself of the information thus collected for some points of history not in my own experience. I have collected from the files of the Philadelphia newspapers of the last century some notes of incidents which may be of interest.

✦⟫⋇⟪✦

OFFICERS OF THE SERVICE

From James Hill Martin's "Bench and Bar" I have taken the following lists of the officers of the quarantine service. I have made a few changes in the dates of the first appointments for Port Physician. This title had only a general sense in the earlier period; it was not until rather late in the eighteenth century that it became the specific title of an official. In early times, there were Resident and Consulting Port Physicians, the former presumably living on Province Island. It ceased to be a State office in 1893.

Facts which will be set forth in the historical note indicate that it was many years before any of these offices acquired the specific character and emoluments that now belong to them.

HEALTH OFFICERS

Spencer Trotter	in office	1754	William Loughlin	appointed	1845
Sylvanus Brown	"	1754	George P. Little	"	1848
Thomas Coombe	"	1761	William McGlensey	"	1852
Peter de Haven	appointed	1779	James W. T. McAllister	"	1855
Henry Dougherty	in office	1780	John H. Henderson	"	1857
John Jones, M.D.	appointed	1780	Arthur Hughes	"	1858
Nathaniel Falconer	"	1780	William Read	"	1861
William Allen	"	1793	George Rush Smith	"	1864
James Philip Pugh	"	1809	Horatio Gates Sickel	"	1865
Nicholas Esling	"	1817	John E. Addicks	"	1866
William Manday	"	1816	James L. Selfridge	"	1883
Samuel K. Franklin	"	1831	Moses Veale	"	1884
Samuel Heintzelman	"	1834	Joseph G. Patterson	"	1887
William Marks	"	1836	Moses Veale		1891
Jarvis Webster	"	1836	Theodore Stull		1895
Peter Rambo	"	1836			

PORT PHYSICIANS

Dr. Patrick Baird	appointed	1720		Dr. Henry Dietrich	appointed	1845
Dr. Thomas Graeme	"	1728		Dr. William Henry	"	1848
Dr. Lloyd Zachary	"	1728		Dr. David Gilbert	"	1852
Dr. Thomas Bond	"	1741		Dr. J. Howard Taylor	"	1855
Dr. James Hutchinson	consulting	1790		Dr. Eliab Ward	"	1856
Dr. Benjamin Rush	resident	1790		Dr. S. P. Brown	"	1858
Dr. James Mease	"	1795		Dr. John F. Trenchard	"	1861
Dr. James Duffield	consulting	1795		Dr. H. Ernest Goodman	"	1867
Dr. J. Redman Coxe	in office	1798		Dr. Walter Atlee Hoffman	"	1873
Dr. James Hall	appointed	1799		Dr. Philip Leidy	"	1874
Dr. Samuel Duffield	"	1800		Dr. Robert H. Alison	"	1883
Dr. John Syng Dorsey	"	1813		Dr. Henry Leffmann	"	1884
Dr. Alexander Knight	"	1814		Dr. William H. Randle	"	1887
Dr. Josiah Steward	"	1827		Dr. Henry Leffmann	"	1891
Dr. William Carll Brewster	"	1831		Dr. Edward O. Shakespeare	"	1892
Dr. John A. Elkinton	"	1836		Dr. Henry C Boenning	"	1893
Dr. Isaac N Marselis	"	1839				

LAZARETTO PHYSICIANS

Dr. Michael Leib	appointed	1800		Dr. Henry Pleasants	appointed	1855
Dr. Nathan Dorsey	"	1805		Dr. J. Howard Taylor	"	1856
Dr. George Buchanan	"	1806		Dr. L. S. Gilbert	"	1858
Dr. Edward Lowber	"	1808		Dr. D. K. Shoemaker	"	1861
Dr. Isaac Hiester	"	1809		Dr. Thomas Stewardson	"	1864
Dr. Thomas Mitchell	"	1813		Dr. George W. Fairlamb	"	1865
Dr. Joel B. Sutherland	"	1816		Dr. William S. Thompson	"	1867
Dr. George F. Lehman	"	1817		Dr. J. Howard Taylor	"	1870
Dr. Joshua W. Ash	"	1836		Dr. D. K. Shoemaker	"	1873
Dr. Wilmer Worthington	"	1839		Dr. W. T. Robinson	"	1878
Dr. Jesse W. Griffiths	"	1842		Dr. F. S. Wilson	"	1884
Dr. Joshua Y. Jones	"	1845		Dr. H. B. Brusstar	"	1887
Dr. James S. Rich	"	1848		Dr. Edwin M Herbst	"	1891
Dr. T. J. P. Stokes	"	1854				

Office changed to " Quarantine Physician " in 1893, and Dr. Henry C Boenning appointed

QUARANTINE MASTERS

Thomas Egger	probably in office	1800		Lewis R. Denin	appointed	1858
Capt. William Lake	in office	1809		Robert Gartside	"	1861
Christopher O'Conner	appointed	1810		Nathan Shaw	"	1864
Capt. Thomas Moore	"	1818		Thomas O. Stevensen	"	1867
Henry Kenyon	"	1819		Robert Gartside	"	1870
Joseph M G Lescure	"	1831		Dr. John H. Gihon	"	1870
Stephen Horne	"	1836		Dr. A. W. Mathews	"	1874
Benjamin Martin	"	1839		Dr. C. C. V. Crawford	"	1879
Alexander McKeever	"	1842		Horace R. Manley	"	1883
Capt. John H Cheyney	"	1848		Robert H. Newhard	"	1887
William V. McKean	"	1852		Patrick Bradley	"	1891
Matthew Van Dusen, Jr.	"	1854		William R. Murphy	"	1892
Jacob Pepper	"	1855				

Office abolished in 1893.

To _____ _____ Lippman _____ Esquire.

Of the County of _Philadelphia_ _____

Sends Greeting:

KNOW YE, that in Trust and Confidence in your Prudence, Integrity and Abilities, I, Robert E. Pattison, Governor as aforesaid, have appointed you the said

_____ _____ Lippman _____ _____ to be

Port _____ _____ of the Port of Philadelphia in this Commonwealth.

You are, therefore, by these presents, appointed and commissioned to be Port _____ as aforesaid vice Robert Barthelow.

To Have and To Hold the said office, together with all the Rights, Powers and Privileges thereunto belonging, or by law in anywise appertaining, until the end of the next session of the Senate.

GIVEN under my Hand and the Great Seal of the State at Harrisburg, this _tenth_ day of _November_ in the year of our Lord one thousand eight hundred and eighty four _____ and of the Commonwealth the one hundred and _ninth_.

By the Governor:

_____ _____ Secretary of the Commonwealth

Fragments of History

Mine is a tale of Flodden Field,
And not a history —

N the eighteenth century Philadelphia was a city of considerable commercial importance, and had trade with all parts of the world. The earliest editions of the newspapers give rather more prominence to the port business than to any other class of local news. In the *American Weekly Mercury*, which was originally a single sheet of rather large octavo size, half a column, at least, is generally given to the shipping news, which is a proportion of about one-eighth of the entire issue. This represented a week's business, and included some notices of arrivals and departures at other ports. I have examined many of these newspapers, beginning with the issues of 1719. It is interesting to note certain differences of phraseology, such as the terms "Entered Inwards" and "Cleared Outwards"; the latter afterward took the form "Cleared Out" and has of late years become simply "Cleared." The name "Snow" occurs quite frequently as the designation of a style of vessel analogous to our modern bark, but having the mizzen-mast smaller. The term "Sloop" also appears quite frequently and in these earlier times the name "Scooner" is correctly spelled. This word is believed to have been derived from the word "to scoon." The Century Dictionary states that the first vessel so called is said to have been built at Gloucester, Mass., by Capt. Andrew Robinson in 1713. As the vessel slid off the ways, a bystander cried out: "Oh, how she scoons!" Robinson instantly replied, "A scooner let her be," and from that time the vessels of this rig have gone by that name. The modern spelling suggests a derivation from German or Dutch, but the names in all languages are from the English.

The following table, taken from the *American Weekly Mercury*, shows the number of vessels in port on Tuesday, December 31, 1728:—

Large ships,	14
Snows, . .	3
Brigantines,	8
Sloops,	9
Scooners,	2

and several small craft.

The "large ships" would be considered small to-day, since one of the regular traders between London and Philadelphia was the Ship *Constantine*, 130 tons.

Other noticeable features of the commercial reports of the last century are the frequent mention of pirates and the slowness in the transmission of news. The damage by pirates was a constant subject of discussion, and it is not infrequent to find in the advertisements of vessels about to sail mention of the fact that they have several guns (cannon) on board and that "the crew can make a tolerable defense." The West India trade seems especially to have suffered from this trouble. Of course, the boldness with which the pirates carried on their work was in part due to want of international comity. The great maritime nations of the world thought it necessary to quarrel with each other and were, therefore, incapable of making a concerted effort against the enemies of honest trade. We should be glad that we live in an age when this narrow and bloodthirsty spirit is declining and nation can join with nation in carrying out the principles of peace and good-will. Nevertheless, the leaven has not yet done its full work, for the events of the last few years have shown that even in a country like the United States, to the happiness of which peace and commercial reciprocity are essential, there are those who would plunge into war merely to gratify ambition, international hate, or avarice. Sometimes good comes out of what seems to be an evil, and the enormous extension of the warlike constructions may soon render war impossible and the twentieth century *may* see the realization of the poet's prophecy of universal federation.

Not the least striking feature of the business life of one hundred years ago is the large infusion of piety into every phase and the frequency of pious allusions. Doctrinal religious beliefs in those days were deeper and more general than to-day. Heinrich Heine standing before one of the great German cathedrals was asked by a friend, "Why can we not erect such structures now?" He replied, "because this was built in an age of convictions; ours is an age of opinions." The uncertainty of life among those who go down to the sea in ships has tended to increase their fervency and anxiety for protection by superhuman influences, and the bills of health, lading, etc., sometimes exhibit this to a high degree. The examples given on the next page are from the archives of The Philadelphia Maritime Exchange.

The slowness in the transmission of intelligence seems to have been due in part to the same want of good feeling between different communities. In these days, when a collision in the harbor of Melbourne is known at Philadelphia in an hour or so, we can scarcely appreciate a condition of affairs under which a serious disaster at Cape Henlopen would not be known at Philadelphia for several days. "We hear from the capes," says the *American Weekly Mercury* of December 10, 1741, "that the Ship *Vernon*, Joseph Redmond, commander, who sailed from this port last week for South Carolina, was on Saturday last lost on the Shears. All Hands are saved." News from New York and Boston was generally more than a week old and foreign news months old. The *American Weekly Mercury* of March 8, 1719-20 contains a letter from London, dated November 23d of the

[Bill of Health]

This bill was issued at New York to the Ship *Penman*, 447 tons, manned by a crew of twenty-six men, and owned by Preserved Fish, a well-known merchant of New York.

To All the Faithful in Christ to Whom These Presents Shall Come:

WHEREAS, It is pious and just to bear witness to the truth, lest error and desert shall overcome it,—

Now, therefore, be it known that the good Ship *Penman*, of which Alexander Coffin, Jr., is Master, having a crew of twenty-six men, is about to sail, if God please, to the port of Canton ;

BE IT KNOWN that (praise be to God the most high and just) no plague or contagion exists at this port.

WITNESS our hands and seals of office, etc.

Dated May 24, 1802.

———— ✣

[Bill of Lading]

SHIPPED, by the Grace of God, in good Order and well conditioned, by Sam'l Clarke, in and upon the good Sloop called the *Betsy*, whereof is Master, under God, for this present voyage, *David Goldsmith*, and now riding at Anchor in the *River Savannah*, and by God's Grace bound for *New York*, to say, *to say :*—

[Here follows list of cargo]

being marked and numbered as in the Margin, and to be delivered in like good Order and well conditioned at the aforesaid Port of *New York* (the Dangers of the Seas only excepted) unto *Joseph Gurnok*, or to his assigns, he or they paying Freight for the said Goods *twelve shillings*, with Primage and Average accustomed.

IN WITNESS WHEREOF, the Master or Purser of said Ship hath affirmed to *two* Bills of Lading, all of this Tenor and Date ; the *one* of which *two* Bills being accomplished, the other *one* to stand void. And so God send the Ship to her desired Port in Safety. Amen.

DAVID GOLDSMITH.

Dated in *Savannah*,
21 October, 1786.

THE "DUTCH" HOSPITAL AT THE LAZARETTO
From a photograph by the author

preceding year, and a notice that in future the post to New York and Boston is to set out weekly. On December 22, 1722, it is stated that during the ensuing season the post will go every two weeks.

The reports contain frequent notices of vessels that were evidently regular traders, among which may be noted the Ship *John*, John Ball, master, which was afterward sunk in Delaware Bay and caused the shoal upon which Ship-John light is built. I am informed by a waterman that the figure-head of the ship is still preserved at the light-house. The uncertainty of navigation is indicated by the advertisements of ships "to sail at the first opportunity." One of the older pilots told me that he remembered a case in which he had been two days taking a vessel from Port Richmond to Washington Street wharf. The want of steam vessels also prevented the breaking up of the ice in the river.

SHIP-JOHN LIGHT

The vessels of those days were small, and when carrying passengers must have been most disagreeably overcrowded; they frequently made very long voyages, and we are not surprised at the amount of disease which was developed on board. The principal diseases were yellow fever, typhus fever, and small-pox. The mortality was often high and there was constant danger of the communication of the diseases to the city. Up to the early part of the nineteenth century scarcely a summer passed without the occurrence of yellow fever in marked form in the sea-board cities. In the Health Law of 1818 small-pox and measles were expressly excepted from the list of diseases for which a vessel might be detained.

The existing records do not clearly indicate how the quarantine service was carried on, but as early as 1700 a law was made entitled, "An Act to prevent sickly vessels coming into this Government." This was continued in force until January 22, 1774. At a session of the Council held at Philadelphia, March 22, 1720, the Governor,

Patrick Gordon Esq. Governour of the Province of Pensilvania & Counties of New Castle, Kent and Sussex upon Delaware.

To Doctor Thomas Graeme & Doctor Lloyd Zachary, Physicians, Sendeth Greeting.

[SEAL.]

Whereas, The Ship Faro,   New, Master, and the Ship Dorothy,   Bedford, Master, both from Bristol in Great Britain, are lately arrived in the River Delaware, and it being very necessary that said ships should be visited before they enter at his Majesties Custom House to the End it may be known if their several Crews together with the Passengers on board are in good health and free from all infectious diseases. These are therefore to authorize and Impower you the said Doctor Thomas Graeme and Doctor Lloyd Zachary to goe on board the said Ships and strictly examine & inspect into the State & Condition of health of there several Crews and of all the passengers on board of which you are to make Report to me on your oath or affirmation. Given under my hand & seal at arms at Philadelphia, the second day of April, in the first year of Reign of our Sovereign Lord King George the second Annoq Domini 1728.

P. GORDON.

Sir William Keith, called attention to the importance of measures to increase the efficiency of this act, and stated that he had prepared the "Draught" of Commission authorizing and directing Patrick Baird, of Philadelphia, chirurgeon, to visit vessels and issue necessary orders. It does not appear that any special title was given to the office, although he would doubtless be alluded to as the Physician of the Port. On April 2, 1728, the Governor commissioned Dr. Thomas Graeme and Dr. Lloyd Zachary to visit certain vessels which were supposed to be infected. As this is the earliest formal commission emanating from the Governor that I have found, I have copied it in full from the Colonial Records. The report of the physicians showed that there was sickness on the *Faro*, but that all were well on the *Dorothy*. The report is endorsed, "Order to visit ships *Dorothy* and *Pharoah*."

Dr. Graeme exercised these functions for many years, being often associated with other physicians. By a minute of Council dated April 2, 1728, it appears that no provision existed at that date for landing the sick, or for vessels stopping at any point for inspection. In 1740 Dr. Graeme rendered an account for visiting and reporting on six Palatine vessels and one with negroes from South Carolina, at a pistole each, a total of £9 16s. Payment was refused for want of evidence as to his authority for acting in this capacity. Next year a bill amounting to £8 8s. for similar services, said to be by order of the Governor, was presented. He was ultimately allowed £10 on these accounts. There was considerable discussion between the local and State authorities on this and other questions connected with the quarantine service, and in consequence of the difficulty of collecting fees some of the physicians declined to visit vessels. Among other things it was asserted that Dr. Graeme had passed a Palatine vessel as in good health and it had introduced disease into the city. It was stated by one of the parties to the discussion that the agitation had been in part started with a view of influencing the elections which were shortly to take place. We can see by this that the "last card" dodge of campaigning was not unknown to our ancestors. The Palatine vessels alluded to above were so called because their passengers were emigrants from the Palatinate in South Germany. They were then commonly known as "Redemptioners," because the expense of their ocean journey was paid by the shipowner, who held them for redemption by the farmers of the vicinity for whom they worked until the passage-money was earned. They settled in Pennsylvania in large numbers, and were the ancestors of that characteristic population now so widely known as the Pennsylvania Dutch.

It will be quite unnecessary to treat in particular detail the incidents of the quarantine in its earlier history, and I pass to the consideration of the establishment of the station. On February 3, 1742–43 (the double date is used in consequence of the two different methods then in vogue for fixing the beginning of the year), an act was passed for vesting in the Commonwealth, the title to Province or State Island and the buildings thereon erected. This island forms the west side of the mouth of the Schuylkill. A portion of the Lazaretto buildings still remains. In 1793–94 vessels were ordered to anchor opposite the island. A Board of Health of Philadelphia was established by an Act passed April 22, 1794. On May 31, 1797, the Board passed a resolution requesting pilots to have the ship-masters hoist a signal on each vessel subject to quarantine duty, in order that the officers at the station might know which vessels to visit. In those days the movements of vessels were either by the wind or rowing, and it was a great annoyance to the officers at the station to make unnecessary trips. In the minutes of the Board, as quoted by Dr. Robinson, this signal is designated a "wiff." The proper form is "waft" (corrupted in nautical usage into wheft or weft) and means a flag rolled up lengthwise with one or more stops. Before the regular signal code was in vogue, a waft at the peak meant a wish to speak to the parties signaled. The term is still in use among watermen of the port of

RESIDENCE OF THE LAZARETTO PHYSICIAN
(From a photograph for the author)

ALONG THE FRONT OF THE STATION

(From a photograph by the author)

Philadelphia, though frequently pronounced "wift," and is understood to mean a flag set at the head of the foremast. With American vessels, the American ensign is usually employed and it is now rarely tied. Foreign vessels mostly use the ordinary square yellow quarantine flag, which is the code symbol for the letter "Q." In New York harbor, at the present time, sailing vessels often set a flag in the side-rigging as a call for the quarantine officer, but in the port of Philadelphia this position of the flag is usually regarded as a call for a tug.

On November 3, 1797, the Board of Health recommended that "an experienced ship-master should reside at the station and visit vessels in company with the physician." This is the origin of the office long designated as Quarantine Master and abolished in 1893. The lazaretto on Province Island became unsatisfactory and on April 24, 1799, a committee reported on available new sites, naming two, Tinicum Island and the river shore below Marcus Hook. The former location was selected, and on January 23, 1800, provision was made for building houses at the station for the Lazaretto Physician and Quarantine Master, respectively. These buildings were in course of construction in 1801, and on February 16th of that year the Board requested the Port Wardens to notify all pilots of the location of the new Lazaretto, and of the requirements of the law in regard to stopping there for inspection. I find in the minutes of the Board of Port Wardens that on February 24th a resolution was adopted to this effect and each pilot was required to sign an acknowledgment that he had received and understood the notice. It took several months before all the pilots then in service had reported at the office. Among the signatures occur the names, Schellinger, Eldridge, and Hughes. Pilots of the same name are to-day on the Port Wardens' roll. Some of the others who signed could only make their mark.

That quarantine work was no sinecure in those days is shown by the report on August 1, 1801, that the Brig *Adventurer* had arrived, reporting fifty-three deaths during the voyage out of a total of one hundred and two passengers and its crew, and that the remainder on board were all sick except the mate. Dr. James Hall, who was evidently very prominent in the service of that time, died September 16, 1801, and at the meeting of the Board held on the 12th of October, a tombstone was ordered for his grave at the Lazaretto; this grave is still to be seen in the cemetery within the bounds of the station. On May 17, 1802, there is a notice of the purchase of a horse and sulky for carrying the mail from the station to the office of the Board. The term "Lazaretto Physician" seems to have been first used as a specific title in 1803. On March 7, 1805, provision was made for the building of the hospital at the back part of the grounds and long known as the Dutch Hospital, because some of the Palatine immigrants were housed there.

Many cases of disease were treated at the Lazaretto during the first half of the present century. A book containing the records from an early period was kept at the Dutch Hospital. I have often been interested in reading the entries.

Dr. Jones, who was Lazaretto Physician from 1845 to 1848, not infrequently took a dozen or more persons from one vessel, and one year he had three hundred patients in the hospital during a month. The large sailing vessels which carried many steerage passengers were especially subject to typhus fever. The West India vessels often brought yellow fever. Cholera occurred at rare intervals, but during the last epidemic of cholera in Philadelphia (1866) only one case was taken off at the Lazaretto and that was from an outgoing vessel. About twenty-five years ago the violence and frequency of ship-diseases began to decline and since 1870 no serious conditions have occurred. In that year an epidemic of yellow fever broke out at the station which caused the death of both the officers and of several other residents besides extending to houses outside the bounds and to Philadelphia.

THE MAIN BUILDING AT THE LAZARETTO

(From a photograph by the author)

"AFTER DINNER," LAZARETTO, SEPTEMBER 30, 1886

(From a photograph by the author)

For two decades after this epidemic, the Lazaretto Physicians had but little to worry them. The prevalence of cholera in Europe in 1883 and several years thereafter caused some excitement on the part of the Board of Health, but it was principally exhibited in the form of an attempt to regulate the importation of old rags. A special effort in this direction was made in relation to the cargo of the American Ship *Lucy A. Nickels*. This ship arrived at the port of New York laden with 5000 bales of Japanese cotton rags taken on board at Kobe, the port of Hiogo, Japan. The voyage had occupied about six months. There was no evidence of the existence of cholera in the district around Hiogo at the time the ship loaded, but it had broken out afterward at Nagasaki, which is several hundred miles distant from Hiogo and on another island. The Health Officer of New York refused to admit the vessel unless the consignees would allow each bale of rags to be subjected to a costly and, as alleged by them, destructive process of disinfection by steam. After disputing over the matter for some time, the consignees discharged the cargo into schooners and brought it to Philadelphia. Through the representations made to the Board of Health of Philadelphia and State Board of Pennsylvania, the rags were forbidden to land and an acrimonious discussion was brought about. The New York Health Officer published a long article to show the dangers of distributing disease by old rags, but almost every instance he cited was of the conveyance of small-pox. Only one doubtful incident of conveying cholera was cited and that was with domestic rags. The careful investigations of the State Board of Health of Massachusetts have shown that the danger of importation of cholera by old rags in bales is so trifling as not to enter seriously into the consideration of quarantine management. The rags were ultimately allowed to go to their destination. Quarantine work dropped into its accustomed routine until the summer of 1892, when the outbreak of cholera in Hamburg set the local health authorities again into activity.

Dr. E. M. Herbst was Lazaretto Physician, and I was serving my second term as Port Physician, rather unwillingly, for I had tendered my resignation during the previous October, but had been induced to withdraw it. In the excitement which was produced by the news from Hamburg, the local health authorities sought the advice of Dr. Shakespeare, who had been abroad some years before at the expense of the United States Government investigating the nature of cholera, and his report—a ponderous volume in the usual style of public documents—had appeared not long before. Dr. Shakespeare's ability as a pathologist and microscopist was unquestioned, but under his advice the Board of Health inaugurated a series of unnecessary and harsh restrictions at the Lazaretto, and entered in a contest with the Lazaretto Physician, who was most unjustly treated. I had for months been dissatisfied with the liability to subordination to the officers of the department and in consequence of that feeling had tendered my resignation in October, 1891, but had withdrawn it at the request of friends. At my request, setting forth in a general way without mentioning names the annoyances of my position, Governor Pattison promptly released me from the office. The first uncalled-for act of the season was the detention, at Dr. Shakespeare's suggestion, of the Steamer *British Princess*, Captain Freeth, from Liverpool, with several hundred passengers, for five days at the Lazaretto, for "observation." There was no reason to regard this vessel as infected. From this time on during the summer, fall, and early winter, to which date the Lazaretto season was extended, a continual dispute was kept up, which so exasperated those interested in the commercial affairs of the port that at the ensuing session of the Legislature they united with the citizens of Delaware County and secured the passage of an act changing the location of the station and depriving the Board of Health of functions which it had exercised for nearly one hundred years.

W. NEALE
Health Officer

E. S. WILSON
Lazaretto Physician

L. M. HERBST
Lazaretto Physician

HENRY LEFFMANN
Port Physician

H. R. MANLEY
Quarantine Master

W. R. MURPHY
Quarantine Master

J. HOWARD TAYLOR
Medical Inspector

THE "VISITOR" IN THE INSIDE CHANNEL AT THE LAZARETTO

From a photograph by the author

Methods of the Service

*A port there is in Ithaca, the haunt
Of Phorcys, Ancient of the Sea.*

QUARANTINE restrictions were first established in the fourteenth century against plague. The bill of health, which is so striking a feature of our modern system, was instituted somewhat later. The term quarantine is derived from the Latin word for forty, this being the period during which ships were detained for observations under the barbarous system in vogue in earlier centuries. The more enlightened methods of modern times have substituted prompt inspection and purification for detention and observation, and in well-conducted ports the service is rarely an annoyance to commerce. Up to a very recent period it has not been possible to do proper medical inspection at night, and accordingly the duties of the officers were exercised from sunrise to sunset, and no person except the pilot was permitted to board an arriving vessel until the quarantine officer had visited it, nor was any other person allowed to leave the vessel until it had been duly certified to be in a good state of health. These principles were fairly carried out in connection with the "Lazaretto" season, but had for many years practically broken down so far as regards the term of service of the Port Physician, namely, from October 1st to May 31st.

When I began my first term, my office was located at South Street wharf; a frame building forming part of the Gloucester-Ferry house, was divided into two communicating rooms, one being occupied by the Port Physician, and the other by the United States

Inspectors of Customs, detailed as Boarding Officers. In the dock in front of the office were moored two steam tugs, the *Visitor* and the *Tench Coxe;* the former was maintained by the City of Philadelphia to convey the quarantine officers from point to point, the latter was in regular commission as one of the United States Revenue Marine to convey similarly the Inspectors of Customs. The *Tench Coxe* at that time was under the command of Lieutenant Munger, with whom was associated Mr. Whitworth as engineer. There was a crew of five men. Two Inspectors of Customs, Mr. James E. Murdoch and Mr. Albert C. Neale, were detailed as Boarding Officers who served, as a rule, on alternate days. The *Visitor* was under command of John T. Springer as pilot, with N. B. Archambault as engineer; Joseph Brooks, fireman; James Wright and Jacob Anderson, deck-hands. The utmost good feeling prevailed between the two services and either boat was used for one or the other purposes as convenience suggested. Although the law required vessels arriving after sunset to anchor in the stream and await the visit of the Port Physician in the morning, the condition of the river was frequently such as to render this unsafe, and it had been for many years the custom for vessels possessing clean bills of health and having no evidence of disease on board to be taken to the dock and the captain and the principal officers to come ashore. The Port Physician was expected to be at his office at 9 A. M. in person or by deputy, and since the usual business of the port closed at 4 P. M. it was not absolutely necessary for him to remain later than that hour. A prompt attention, however, to business required an earlier beginning and a later ending of the day's duties, and the officers of the customs-service on all business days began their work at 7 A. M. and continued it until near sunset. Owing to the great advance in sanitary methods among civilized nations and the limited character of the commerce of Philadelphia, there was really very little for the Port Physician to do, except to make out a formal certificate for presentation at the Health Office, which, upon payment of the fee, issued the permit for the entry of the vessel. The laws of Congress subordinate all Federal officers in time of peace to the local quarantine authorities, and hence no vessel from a foreign port was permitted to make entry at the Customs-House until this health certificate had been issued. A century ago, the district including the Gulf States was far more liable to yellow fever than at present, and the Pennsylvania law made vessels from this district, that is, south of St. Mary's River, subject to quarantine supervision at all times. In the summer season the limits were extended as far north as the Cape Fear River. With this exception, vessels from domestic ports were not subject to quarantine duty. Many vessels were passed by the Port Physician without being visited, the captain simply reporting at the office and answering the questions of the Bill of Inquiry. The Bill of Inquiry was a rather imposing document of yellow paper, foolscap size, containing twenty questions which were supposed to cover all important points affecting the health of the vessel during its voyage, or the health of the port from which it came. As an evidence of the condition of the latter the masters usually presented a bill of health which was surrendered to the Port Physician and duly stowed away on an upper shelf to gather dust until its room was needed for other similar documents when the older ones were thrown away. With the approval of Major Veale, Health Officer, I changed the form of certificate to a compact slip upon which was entered merely such data as were needed for the classification of the arrivals, and I succeeded in abolishing forever, so far as the Port Physician is concerned, "the game of twenty questions," which had been in vogue for many years.

The only serious difficulty I found in the carrying out of the duties was the irregularity. The arrival of a vessel is a very uncertain matter. With the magnificent express steamers that have been built of recent years the journey is timed almost with the exactness of railroad service ; but most steam vessels and all sailing vessels are subject to so many interfering conditions that their arrival can only be approximated. The port of Philadelphia is placed under some disadvantages. It is over one hundred miles from the sea to the wharves. Strong winds and low tides may cause considerable delay. Heavy ice may be for days a serious barrier. So far as the freight service is concerned, the business of the port had adjusted itself to these uncertainties, but transatlantic steamers were not permitted to discharge steerage passengers until the vessel had been duly inspected by the Port Physician. This often caused many hours of delay and

BREAKWATER REPORTING STATION

uncertainty, and I have not infrequently waited during the greater part of a day for the arrival of such a vessel.

The convenience of the service was much increased by the courtesy of The Philadelphia Maritime Exchange, which promptly furnished to the Port Physician's office, without charge, its telegraphic reports of the movements of arriving vessels. There were two regular reporting stations, Breakwater and Newcastle. Vessels frequently passed the former during the night and were not distinguished as to name, but

JAMES F. MURDOCH
Inspector of Customs

ALBERT ADAMS
Inspector of Customs

JOHN J. S. RODGERS
Commissioner of Immigration

THEODORE LYNN
Inspector of Customs

(THE LATE) ALBERT C. NEALL
Inspector of Customs

JOHN T. SPRINGER   EZRA D. KELLER

JOSEPH J. BROOKS   N. B. ARCHAMBAULT   JACOB ANDERSON

GEORGE DOUGHERTY   JAMES WRIGHT

CREW OF THE "VISITOR"

as they usually passed Newcastle during daylight they were reported in time to be met on arrival. The regular passenger steamers almost invariably signaled the Breakwater in passing, and thus their coming was known hours before they reached the port. In the ice season a station was usually opened at Chester. At present the reporting stations are Breakwater, Reedy Island, and Marcus Hook.

The telegraphic information was transmitted to me at irregular

MARCUS HOOK REPORTING STATION

intervals during the day, the news being manifolded and a copy of one of these left by the messenger. These manifolds were usually written by the assistant secretary of the Maritime Exchange, Mr. Elisha Crowell. I present specimens of them representing, respectively, a busy day and a dull one. The information received at the Exchange was displayed upon bulletin-boards and when we were impatiently awaiting arrivals, we made frequent calls at the Exchange to get the latest news.

The very uncertainty of the service gave it some interest, but when important vessels were detained by fog and ice, the delay became sometimes too tedious to be agreeable. The arrival of each bulletin from the Maritime Exchange was awaited impatiently, the disappointment which these sometimes occasioned being quite depressing. I remember more than one occasion on which, late in some winter afternoon, when the Commissioner of Immigration, the Boarding Officer, and myself had been for hours waiting for some tidings of a passenger steamer that had been reported as passing the Capes in the morning, we would see the messenger, and quickly taking from him the copy of the manifold would read the following interesting (!) information: " Chester 4 P. M., fog. Steamer *Aries* down."

During the latter part of my first term Mr. James E. Murdoch was on duty on all weekdays as Boarding Officer, and as I enjoyed his company very much, I went with him often, using either the *Visitor* or *Tench Coxe*, as convenient. When we passed each other on our respective boats, we exchanged a signal similar to that by which the wacht-meester of Rensellearstein acknowledged the proclamation of Walter the Testy.

During the interval between my terms, changes occurred in the different services. Some of these were merely incidents of the political upheavals, others were in pursuance of the custom of the departments. Mr. Theodore Lynn and Mr. Albert Adams were Boarding Officers during my second term; Lieut. Munger had been succeeded by Lieut. Washington C. Coulson, prior to the close of my first term, and when I returned to the office, Lieut. John Brann was in command of the revenue boat. I am indebted to all these officers for affording me many facilities, especially when the *Visitor* was out of service, and I have passed many pleasant hours with them in the cabin of the *Tench Coxe*. On the *Visitor*, Capt. Keller had succeeded Capt. Springer, Mr. Brooks had been transferred to another boat and Mr. George Dougherty added to the list.

My position afforded me an excellent opportunity to study the conditions of the sailor's life, for I was, of course, privileged to examine any part of the ship and to see all those on board. Every one knows that a sailor's life is hard and dangerous, but few realize how near to slavery it is. Philanthropy has busied itself with many reforms, all of which are laudable, but there is certainly a wide field for improvements in the condition of the "man before the mast." His quarters are sometimes not as good as those of a valuable animal, and the conditions of service are humiliating in the extreme. Governments have interfered to a certain extent, but much of the legislation is half-hearted and does not secure substantial reform. The condition of the steerage passenger is also a sad one. Here again legislative action has remedied some of the worst evils, but much remains to be done.

The stringency of the immigration laws has been steadily increasing for a dozen years. When I went on duty, in 1884, the examination of incoming passengers of all types was under the State jurisdiction and was somewhat formal. Afterward the United States Government took charge of it and it became more and more exacting. At the present time the immigrants are landed in commodious quarters at the wharf, and no one is permitted to depart until the officers of the Immigration Bureau have

> "Discussed his lineage, told his name,
> His following, and his warlike fame."

I want to offer here testimony to the efficiency of Mr. John J. S. Rodgers, who has been United States Commissioner of Immigration at the Port of Philadelphia for many years. I have had much opportunity to observe men in many departments of official life, but I have seen no one carry out his duties with more justice, fairness, and fidelity than Mr. Rodgers. His duties were far more extended than my own and in many cases decision was more difficult. He seemed to me to combine in the most happy manner the *suaviter in modo* with *fortiter in re*. In saying this I am not wishing to disparage by comparison other officers in associated services, for work in other fields was also well done.

Life at the quarantine station was usually dull. The arrivals averaged about four per day, and when the flood-tide was during the morning, business was generally over by noon. The hours of duty were from sunrise until sunset. In the early part of the quarantine season this was considered to be from 4.30 A. M. to 7.30 P. M. From sunrise until sunset, the half-hours were rung by the bells after the nautical method, and the members of the boat's crew took turns in two-hour watches. The one to whom the early morning watch fell was expected to get out a little before sunrise and ring up the station if any vessel was waiting. The signal for a vessel was three times three bells. The morning visits had become quite frequent, however, since many steamers would continue on their journey up the river during the night, and almost all vessels towing would do the same. Everything that was subject to visit would, of course, wait until after sunrise, and a trip on the river in the early morning was usually very pleasant, and in the warmer season of the year was likely to be the most agreeable part of the day. It gave us an appetite for breakfast, at any rate, and as this was generally served at four bells (six o'clock) and dinner at eight bells (twelve o'clock), we often had long periods of idleness, and it was necessary to resort to some harmless amusement to kill time. The intention was to isolate the station from communication of the surrounding territory, but the actual system fell short of this in more than one respect. In fact, in my first term I learned that about the only things strictly quarantined were the boat and its crew. Later the discipline became somewhat more stringent, though at all times there was a miscellaneous coming and going on the part of some of the members of the board and their friends, which was not in accordance with the main-

THE BOARD ROOM AT SIXTH AND SANSOM STREETS

From a photograph by Mr. R. V. P. Turner

FIRST STEPS ON AMERICAN SOIL
LANDING OF IMMIGRANTS FROM STEAMER ILLINOIS
From a photograph by the author

tenance of the best discipline. The station was a rather convenient
resort for some of the city officials who desired to take advantage of
the gunning season. The population of a quarantine station should
be reduced to a minimum and include only those persons absolutely
needed for the conduct of work, yet I have known as many as forty
people to be at the Lazaretto at one time.

The officers of the station made an official report every day. The
Quarantine Master put these and other papers intended to be for-
warded to the city, into the mail-bag, and in the early morning this
was taken by a messenger to the office of the Board of Health. Any
applications to leave the station or requests for visitors to enter were
recorded in the letter of the Lazaretto Physician. To this letter a
formal reply was always made by the Secretary of the Board, and
the action of the Board upon the requests was noted. The Quarantine Master's report did not receive so much consideration. It was
disposed of by almost a set form of words. After the letter of the
Lazaretto Physician had been read, the presiding officer would say,
" Also a letter from the Quarantine Master, of like import, which will
go on file." In spite of this somewhat cavalier treatment, it is a tra-
dition of the office that on one occasion the Quarantine Master
omitted his letter but was promptly called to account. In later years
of the station, the introduction of the telephone practically deprived
the mail service of much of its interest, since all important communi-
cations were made by the former. I was but rarely at the station and
only for a day or two at a time as a matter of accommodation to
the Lazaretto Physician. Still, one day was so much like the other
that this limited experience gave me an idea of the character of the
life. The station had some disadvantages of location and arrangement,—the land was low and marshy ; the buildings old-fashioned and
inconvenient ; the grounds were very poorly lighted and after dark
there was very little comfort or opportunity for enjoyment. While
conservatism of the Board of Health was in some respects quite

marked and a general indifference to the convenience of the officers
noticeable, the relations between the officers and the Board, though
distant and formal, were not usually unpleasant.

[Samples of Telegraphic Dispatches]

Breakwater, June 13
Thur. 70 S.W. ten miles. cloudy, Barometer 29.10
10 pm Sour. 10⁴⁵ Steamer up, 11 pm tow out, midnight
Barges Moonbeam + David Crockett under Pioneer arriving
I am Br Stm Woodland from Liverpool up, 3am foreig.
Steamer, 3³⁰ Tanker up, 5³⁰ Scw R. + J. Hargraves up.

Breakwater noon - N.W. very light. hazy
Blk Rowlenbuck out, Coast Steamer up-

To determine from these dispatches the time of arrival, it was
necessary to allow for the influence of wind and tide, especially the
latter. I found much interest in studying out the phenomena of the
tides. I had known, from boyhood, of course, that the ebb and flow
occurred every twelve hours, but I learned very early in my service
that it is a wave motion and that it is easy for a vessel to keep in
the flood-tide from the Capes to the port, but impossible to carry
the ebb-tide from the port to the Capes. In fact, both the high water
and low water move *up* the stream, the former being the crest and
the latter the trough of the tidal wave.

THE BEACH PATROL

Pilots and Pilotage

The inhabitants of Zidon and Arvad were thy rowers; thy wise men,
O Tyre, were in thee, they were thy pilots.

THE office of pilot has been in vogue for a long time:
indeed, it is probably coeval with the first maritime
ventures. Its long existence and special nature have
developed it into something of the nature of a caste,
several generations of the same family being found in
the service. The function is, as a rule, an exclusive one, the pilot
limiting his services to a particular harbor. In the Delaware River
pilot system certain names occur over long periods. Among these
are Maull, Marshall, Eldridge, Schellinger, and Hughes.

Some pilots have perpetuated their memories in a rather unenvi-
able way, that is, by having dangerous spots in the harbor named
after them. 'Miah Maull shoal perpetuates the memory of Nehemiah
Maull, pilot of many years ago, and Dan Baker shoal, which has
figured so largely in the discussions of the improvement of the Delaware River, was also named from a pilot.

"If ancient tales say true," pilots occasionally discovered shoals
by the simple method of running vessels on them, but I am not
aware that either of the instances just cited is of this character.

An interesting memento of the "times that tried men's souls"
is preserved in the library of the Historical Society of Pennsylvania.
It is the broadside containing a notice to the pilots not to bring
into port the ship containing the taxed tea. It is too long to quote
in full here: a few extracts will suffice to show its character.

TO THE

DELAWARE PILOTS

We took the pleasure some days since of kindly admonishing you *to do your Duty* if perchance you should meet with the (*Tea*) SHIP POLLY, CAPTAIN AYRES, a THREE-DECKER, which is hourly expected.

We have now to add that Matters ripen fast here, and that *much is expected from those Lads who meet with the Tea Ship.* There is some Talk of A HANDSOME REWARD FOR THE PILOT WHO GIVES THE FIRST GOOD ACCOUNT OF HER. . . . . How that may be we cannot for *certain* determine; but ALL agree that TAR and FEATHERS will be his Portion who pilots her into this HARBOUR. * * * * *

THE COMMITTEE FOR TARRING & FEATHERING.

Nov. 27, 1773.

Pilots usually cruise in small sailing vessels strongly and trimly built, formerly managed by apprentices to the service but now in charge of permanent crews. Each boat carries a few fully qualified pilots and these are put on vessels in turn. A vessel is obliged to take a pilot from the boat which first hails it, and hence the boats often cruise far out to sea in order to secure large vessels that are expected. The pilots of New York harbor have been known to go 700 miles to the north-east or many miles to the southward, seeking for the large steamers that are constantly arriving in that port. New York pilots have begun to use steam-tugs and no longer cruise far from shore. In the last half dozen years, foreign commerce has gone so largely into steamers that there is more certainty in arrivals, and pilots probably lose less time in cruising.

A PILOT-BOAT

From a painting by Gerald Essex

OFF THE CAPES

From a painting by Geo. L. Foote

Compulsory pilotage exists in most ports; *i. e.*, if a pilot speaks a vessel arriving from foreign port, the master thereof is bound to pay for the pilotage to the harbor, whether he takes the pilot or not. This seems at first sight to be unjust, but it is a law growing out of the nature of pilotage duty. The service is perilous and often exceedingly severe, and it can be properly discharged only by men thoroughly trained in the work and intending to devote the best part of their lives to it. To pilot a large vessel into port is a most responsible duty. It is not merely following the channel, for with the modern aids to navigation, range lights, buoys, etc., this is not difficult; but a perfect knowledge of the tides and currents, and of the movements of the many vessels encountered in the harbor is required, and a great loss of life and money may result with a vessel handled by an inexperienced person. Hence it is necessary for the service to be so arranged that there is an assurance of revenue, and as many masters would be tempted for economy's sake to bring their vessels into port without a pilot, imperiling not only their own vessels but others, the principle of compulsory pilotage has been established.

The pilot-apprentice serves six years, being taken many times up the river in company with a fully qualified pilot. He is then examined, and if he shows proficiency is given a "twelve-foot branch," that is, the right to bring into port vessels not drawing over twelve feet of water. After eighteen months' service he is again examined, and if he passes, is licensed to take charge of any vessel that can enter the port. We thus see that while it takes four years to make a doctor, it takes nearly eight to make a pilot.

The compensation is regulated by the draft of the vessel, that is, the depth to which it is loaded, so that it is in proportion to the difficulty and responsibility of the task. The pilot that conducts a vessel into port has the right to take it to sea, and the latter is often the greater duty, for outgoing cargoes are generally heavier than the incoming ones. He leaves the vessel at the Capes, being received by the "take-off" boat, the pilot-boats being assigned in turn to this duty. On rare occasions the weather has been such as to prevent the pilot leaving his vessel and he has been obliged to go with it to the destination. In this way a pilot has made an involuntary trip to Liverpool. He is entitled to a *per diem* compensation under such circumstances. He is also entitled to pay for detentions occurring in his usual work by causes not personal to himself, but he must risk the delays due to wind and tide.

The changed conditions brought about by the large development of steamer traffic have led to modifications of the pilot service. Many steamers discharge cargoes in whole or in part at New York and come to this port to load. The prompt telegraphic service enables news of these charters to be communicated to all the maritime exchanges, and as a vessel leaving New York for Philadelphia must take a New York pilot to Sandy Hook and a Delaware River pilot from the Breakwater to Philadelphia, it became some years ago the custom for certain Philadelphia pilots to go to New York by train, board the vessel and take charge of it as soon as it entered Delaware Bay, thus not only avoiding the trouble of cruising but the uncertainty of securing the vessel. Naturally this led to comment and opposition; those who followed the practice were dubbed "parlor-car pilots." The Board of Port Wardens, which has charge of the administration of pilotage laws, interfered and made rules that require the pilots needed for such purpose to be selected in turn, so that all may have a chance.

Liebe, wir hassen, wir streiten, es trennet uns Neigung und Meinung,
Aber es bleichet indeß dir sich die Locke, wie mir.

www.ingramcontent.com/pod-product-compliance
Lightning Source LLC
Chambersburg PA
CBHW021521090426
42739CB00007B/715